ENGLISH IN ACTION

THIRD EDITION

NATIONAL GEOGRAPHIC
L E A R N I N G

BARBARA H. FOLEY
ELIZABETH R. NEBLETT

Australia · Brazil · Mexico · Singapore · United Kingdom · United States

National Geographic Learning,
a Cengage Company

English in Action Level 3: Third Edition
Barbara H. Foley, Elizabeth R. Neblett

Publisher: Sherrise Roehr

Executive Editor: Sarah Kenney

Managing Development Editor:
Claudienma Mimó

Senior Development Editor:
Lewis Thompson

Associate Development Editor: Katie Davis

Assistant Editor: Becky Long

Media Researcher: Leila Hishmeh

Director of Global Marketing: Ian Martin

Product Marketing Manager: Dalia Bravo

Sr. Director, ELT & World Languages:
Michael Burggren

Production Manager: Daisy Sosa

Content Project Manager: Beth Houston

Manufacturing Customer Account Manager:
Mary Beth Hennebury

Composition: MPS North America LLC

Cover/Text Design: Lisa Trager

Art Director: Brenda Carmichael

Cover Image: ©Jean Pierre Lescourret/
Getty Images

For permission to use material from this text or product,
submit all requests online at **cengage.com/permissions**
Further permissions questions can be emailed to
permissionrequest@cengage.com

Student Edition:
ISBN: 978-1-337-90596-1

Student Edition + OWB:
ISBN: 978-1-337-90687-6

National Geographic Learning
20 Channel Center Street
Boston, MA 02210
USA

Locate your local office at **international.cengage.com/region**

Visit National Geographic Learning online at **NGL.Cengage.com/ELT**
Visit our corporate website at **www.cengage.com**

Printed in China
Print Number: 01 Print Year: 2018

ACKNOWLEDGMENTS

The authors and publisher would like to thank the following reviewers and Advisory-Panel members:

Karin Abell
Durham Technical Community College, Durham, NC

Angela Addy
Passaic County Community College, Passaic, NJ

Beth Anglin
Bucks County Community College, Newtown, PA

Irma Baack
Harper College, Schaumburg, IL

Teresita Bautista
Paramount Adult Education, CA

Rod Bennett
Emily Griffith Technical College, Denver, CO

Anne Bertin
Union County College, New Jersey

Patricia Bone
Montgomery College, Rockville, MD

Carlo Buzzi
North Shore Community College, Danvers, MA

Julia Cantu
MiraCosta College, Oceanside, CA

Fang Chen
Central New Mexico Community College, Albuquerque, NM

Kathryn Clark
Daytona State College, Daytona Beach, FL

Lin Cui
William Rainey Harper College, Palatine, IL

Andre DeSandies
Union County College, New Jersey

Lois Eisenber
Bucks County Community College, Newtown, PA

Linda Foster
Hillsborough County, FL

Tracy Fung
Palomar College, San Marcos, CA

Litsa Georgiou
Union County College, New Jersey

Deborah Greene
Sharon Technical College, Hollywood, FL

Jill Harold
University of North Texas, Denton, TX

Harriet Hirschfeld
Bucks County Community College, Newtown, PA

Katherine Hiscock
Portland Adult Education, Portland, ME

Lorraine Hromalik
Bowers/Whitley Adult Community School, Tampa, FL

Liz Hughes
Rosie's Place, Boston, MA

Dawn Humphry
University of Arkansas Cossatot Community College, Nashville, AR

Kim Johnson
Palomar College, San Marcos, CA

Christopher Kilmer
Emily Griffith Technical College, Denver, CO

Eileen Krai
Bucks County Community College, Newtown, PA

Caron Lieber
Palomar College, Fallbrook, CA

Mayra Lopez
MiraCosta College, Oceanside, CA

Melissa Lutz
University of Arkansas Cossatot Community College, De Queen, AR

Diann Mandile
Emily Griffith Technical College, Denver, CO

Cheo Massion
College of Marin, Kentfield, CA

Lynn Meng
Union County College, New Jersey

Gregor Mieder
Metropolitan State University, Denver, CO

Susan Moser
Portland Community College, Portland, OR

Susana Murillo
Palomar College, San Marcos, CA

Karen Nelson
Pittsburg State University, Pittsburg, KA

Sergei Paromchik
Hillsborough County Public Schools, Tampa, FL

Claudia Pena
Houston Community College, Houston, TX

Dinah Perren
Palomar College, Oceanside, CA

Kandyce Pinckney
Emily Griffith Technical College, Denver, CO

Howard Pomann
Union County College, New Jersey

Nicole Powell
SUNY Orange, Bloomingburg, NY

Tami Richey
Palomar College, San Marcos, CA

Julie Roberts
Georgia Piedmont Technical College, Doravilla, GA

Christi Stilley
CARIBE Refugee Program, Tampa, FL

Gail Voorhes
Palomar College, Ramona, CA

Huaxin Xu
Union County College, New Jersey

Rochelle Yanike-Hale
Portland Adult Education, Portland, ME

Beth Zarret
Bucks County Community College, Newtown, PA

Miriam Zemen
Montgomery College, Silver Spring, MD

CONTENTS

Contents   **v**

CONTENTS

First-year students move into
Victoria College, in Toronto, Canada.

ACADEMIC Take notes; interpret graphs;
take a survey

AT WORK Introduce yourself and others;
read and interpret visuals; identify strengths and
weaknesses

CIVICS Understand classroom expectations

A Read.

Hi. My name is Kenji, and I'm a student at the University of California, San Diego. I'm a student in the English language program. I'm taking Listening and Pronunciation in Room 142. There are ten students in my class, four men and six women. We are from five different countries. Our class meets on Mondays, Wednesdays, and Fridays from 10:30 a.m. to 12:30 p.m. My teacher is Ms. Burak. Her office is in Room 12.

B Complete the sentences about yourself.

1. My name is _____.
2. I'm a student at _____.
3. I'm taking _____ in Room _____.
4. There are _____ students in my class, _____ men and _____ women.
5. I have class on _____.
    days
6. My teacher is _____. His / Her office is in Room _____.

C **ACADEMIC** Listen to Gloria interview Kenji about his life in the United States. Take notes. Then, compare your notes with a partner. 🎧2

WRITING STRATEGY
When you take notes, you write a few words to help you remember important information. You do not write full sentences.

Kenji:

Japan

six months

D Look at your notes. Answer the questions about Kenji.

1. What country is Kenji from? He's from Japan.
2. How long has he been in the United States?
3. Why is he in the United States?
4. How many people are in his family?
5. Where does he live?
6. Is he a new student?
7. Does he work?
8. Is he married?
9. How old is he?
10. How often does he swim?
11. What other interests does he have?
12. What kind of music does he like?
13. What kind of computer does he have?
14. How will he meet other students at college? What do you think?

CULTURE NOTE
Americans usually do not ask about age or religion when they first meet a person. They do not talk about their salary with strangers or friends, and sometimes not even with family.

I **am** a student. I **live** in New York. I **work** part time. I **have** a computer.	She **is** a student. She **lives** in New York. She **works** part time. She **has** a computer.	They **are** students. They **live** in New York. They **work** part time. They **have** computers.

A Complete the sentences.

1. Eva and Mariola (be) _____ are _____ sisters.
2. They (study) _____ English at Summit Adult School.
3. Eva (work) _____ full time.
4. Mariola (have) _____ two small children.
5. They (go) _____ to school two nights a week.
6. Eva (drive) _____ to school.
7. She (pick up) _____ Mariola on the way to school.
8. On the way to school, they (talk) _____ about their families.

B In your notebook, write ten sentences about Pierre.

Name:	Pierre Dorval
Age:	32
Country:	Haiti
Years in US:	Four
School:	Bay Adult School; Intermediate level; Mondays and Wednesdays, 9:00 a.m to 12:00 p.m.
Marital Status:	Married, one son
Occupation:	Waiter; West Hotel; six nights a week
Interests:	Soccer and guitar
Computer:	Yes
Music:	Jazz and rock

C **LET'S TALK.** Interview a classmate. Take notes.

1. What's your name? _____
2. What country are you from? _____
3. Is your family here in the United States? _____
4. How many people are in your family? _____
5. How long have you been in the United States? _____
6. Where do you live? _____
7. Are you a new student in this school? _____
8. How do you get to school? _____
9. Do you have a driver's license? _____
10. Are you married? Do you have any children? If so, how many?
    _____
11. Do you work? Where do you work? What do you do?
    _____
12. What are your interests? _____
13. What kind of music do you like? _____
14. Do you have a computer? _____

D **AT WORK** **LET'S TALK.** Introduce your partner to the class.

I'd like you to meet Gloria. She's from Guanajuato, Mexico. She lives here in Los Angeles. She's . . .

Guanajuato, Mexico.

ACTIVE GRAMMAR | *There is / There are* and Prepositions

There	is isn't	a library	**in** this building. **in** this school.
	are aren't	restrooms	**on** this floor.

More information in Appendix A.

A **ACADEMIC** Complete the sentences about the school map. Use the prepositions in the box.

| Elevator | 👩 | 👨 | 🖥 205 Computer lab | 🖥 | 207 | 210 Library |
| Stairs | | 202 | 204 Nurse | 206 | 208 | |

1. The library is _____*at the end of*_____ the hall.
2. The nurse's office is _____ Room 204.
3. There is an elevator _____ the stairs.
4. The women's restroom is _____ Room 202.
5. The library is _____ the second floor.
6. The stairs are _____ the hall.
7. The men's restroom is _____ the women's restroom.
8. There are a few computers _____ the library.
9. There is also a computer lab _____ this floor.
10. There are many computers _____ the computer lab.

> **at the end of** the hall
> **in** Room 201
> **on** the second floor
> **next to** the stairs
> **across from** Room 202

B Circle the rooms and facilities in your school.

ATM	copy machine	library	swimming pool
bookstore	counselor's office	nurse's office	theater
cafeteria	day care center	restrooms	tutoring center
computer lab	gym	student center	water fountains

C **LET'S TALK.** Use *there is* and *there are* to describe the facilities at your school.

> There's a tutoring center in the library.

D Answer the questions about your school.

1. Is this school in a city?
2. Is this school large?
3. Is this school open in the evening?
4. Are there many students in this school?
5. Are there many computers in this classroom?
6. Is there a library in this building?
7. Is the library open today?
8. Is there a water fountain on this floor?
9. Are there any restrooms on this floor?
10. Is there a cafeteria in this building?
11. Is the cafeteria's food good?
12. Is there a bookstore in this building?
13. Are the books expensive?
14. Are the students friendly?
15. Are the students from many different countries?

> Is there a library in this building?
> Yes, there is.
> No, there isn't.

> Is this school small?
> Yes, it is.
> No, it isn't.

> Are there any restrooms on this floor?
> Yes, there are.
> No, there aren't.

> Are the students friendly?
> Yes, they are.
> No, they aren't.

E **Pronunciation: Sentence stress** Listen and repeat. Then, listen again and underline the stressed words. 🎧3

1. The cafeteria is on the first floor.
2. The nurse's office is across from the elevator.
3. The bookstore is in the student center.
4. The computer lab is on the third floor.
5. There is a copy machine in the library.
6. The restrooms are next to the stairs.

> The important words in a sentence receive stress. We say these words a little more clearly and give them a little more emphasis.

1. **All of** the students study English.

2. **Many of** the students have computers.

3. **Some of** the students work.

4. **A couple of** the students are married.

5. **One of** the students wears glasses.

6. **None of** the students has a cat.

A Circle the correct verb.

1. Many of us **is / are** from Spanish-speaking countries.
2. Ten of the students **work / works** part time.
3. Most of the students **have / has** computers.
4. One of the students **take / takes** the train to school.
5. None of us **live / lives** in a dormitory.

WORD PARTNERSHIPS	
a couple	
a few	
all	
most	of us
none	of them
one	of the students
some	
ten	

B AT WORK The graph shows how students in one class get to school. Look at the graph and answer the questions.

1. How many students are in the class?
2. How do most students get to school?
3. How many students take the bus?
4. How many students walk?

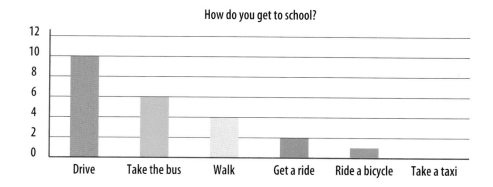

C Write five sentences about the graph in Exercise B.

1. _Ten of the students drive_ _____ to school.
2. _____ to school.
3. _____ to school.
4. _____
5. _____
6. _____

D ACADEMIC **LET'S TALK.** Survey your classmates. Then, complete the graph. In your notebook, write five sentences about the information. Use *all of us*, *many of us*, *some of us*, and so on.

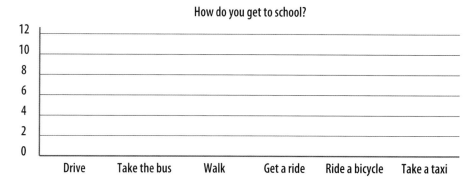

A Classroom expectations vary from country to country. Read each statement. Circle the information that is true for your country.

1. In some countries, students can arrive a few minutes late for class.
2. In some places, students call the teacher "Teacher," not by his or her name.
3. In some countries, textbooks are free.
4. In many countries, students sit quietly, listen to the teacher, and take notes.
5. In most countries, students raise their hands to ask or answer a question.
6. In some countries, students stand when they speak.
7. In some places, students can bring a cup of coffee into the classroom.
8. In most places, students have to turn off their cellphones before class.
9. In some countries, students have many hours of homework.
10. In some countries, students can copy each other's homework.
11. In a few countries, students do group projects and assignments.

These are students of English as a second language.

B | CIVICS | Listen to each statement. Circle *True* if the statement is true for your class. Circle *False* if it is false for your class. 🎧4

1. True	False	**7.** True	False
2. True	False	**8.** True	False
3. True	False	**9.** True	False
4. True	False	**10.** True	False
5. True	False	**11.** True	False
6. True	False	**12.** True	False

C Write three more expectations in your classroom.

1. _____

2. _____

3. _____

D Ask your teacher these questions about your school and your class.

1. Where is your office?

2. Can I email you? What is your email address?

3. Does this school have a computer lab? Can I get a student account?

4. May I bring a computer to class?

5. Is there a library in this school? How do I get a library card?

6. Do we have homework every night?

7. What should I do if I don't understand something?

8. What are we going to study in this class?

9. Are there other classes I can take at this school?

10. What should I do if I am absent?

11. What is the school calendar? Do we have any vacation days?

E Write three more questions about your school or class. Then, ask your teacher the questions.

_____

_____

_____

A Underline the problem(s) each student is having with English.

English Is Frustrating!

Ravi

I work 50 hours a week as a taxi driver, so I talk to people all day. They understand me, but I know I make a lot of mistakes. No one corrects me. My vocabulary is strong. Grammar is my problem. For example, I don't use the simple past. I always say, "I drive him to the office this morning" instead of "I drove him to the office this morning." I'm trying to change little by little.

Maria Luisa

I live in an area where everyone speaks Spanish. I can speak Spanish with my neighbors and friends, at the supermarket, at the bank, and at the post office. I don't work, so it's really difficult to find ways to practice English.

Lian

I understand the grammar and the readings in my class. I think my writing is good, but I'm very nervous when I speak English. I don't want to make any mistakes because people will think that I'm not smart. Also, my pronunciation isn't good. When I speak, people often say, "What? Say that again."

Ketsia

I have been in the United States for one year. I'm studying hard and I'm learning grammar, but the vocabulary is difficult. When I listen, I don't understand many of the words. When I try to read, there are two or three new words in every sentence. I feel bad about it. 🎧5

B Read the suggestions for learning English. Add one more suggestion.

1. Watch one TV show in English every day.
2. Listen to songs in English. Sing along.
3. Try to speak English when you go out in the community.
4. Use the internet or an app. There are many English learning tools online.
5. Don't worry about mistakes. It's natural to make mistakes when you are learning a language.
6. Use English language learning computer programs in your computer lab.
7. Find a study partner. Work together one or two days after school.
8. Make a friend from your school who doesn't speak your language. Meet once a week after class for conversation practice.
9. Read the newspaper in English.
10. Be kind to yourself. Understand that learning another language takes time.
11. Keep an English journal. Write a mistake you made while speaking. Then, write the sentence correctly. Also, write new words and sentences you hear.
12. _____

C Give each student on the previous page two or three suggestions from the list in Exercise B. Write the numbers of the suggestions on the lines next to their names.

Ravi _____4_____ _____ _____

Maria Luisa _____ _____ _____

Lian _____ _____ _____

Ketsia _____ _____ _____

D **AT WORK** Write two of your strengths in learning English. Write two of your difficulties. Which suggestions can you try?

My Strengths   My Difficulties

_____   _____

_____   _____

1. I'm going to _____.
2. I'm going to _____.

**Many words used in English come from other languages.
Yoga and sushi are two examples. What words from your
language are used in English?**

A Read Sandra's story. She is introducing herself to her teacher and class.

Start your story on the front of the paper.

Give your story a title.
Write the title in the middle of the line.

Buses arrive at the Museo del Oro (Gold Museum) bus stop in Bogota, Colombia.

Hello

Skip a line between the title and the story.

My name is Sandra and I am from Bogota, Colombia. I came to the United States five years ago. My sister, Gloria, is here with me, but my mom and dad and my six brothers all live in Colombia. I miss them a lot, but we email each other all the time.

Indent each paragraph.

I work full time at a small printing company. I do several jobs at this company. Sometimes, I do data entry. At other times, I help customers at the counter.

I don't have much free time, but I enjoy music, especially rock and romantic music. On Saturday afternoons, I play tennis with the tennis club at my school.

Right now, I'm studying English. I plan to major in communications and work in the TV industry. I have many dreams. Someday, I would like to live in Florida and have a family.

Put your name and the date at the top or bottom of your composition.

Sandra Martinez, September 10

B Look at Sandra's composition and complete her notes.

My Family	My Work	My Interests	My Future
Gloria	printing company		
six brothers	full time		
Mom and Dad	data entry		
	help customers		

C Correct the mistakes with the articles, and the singular and plural nouns.

1. I have two ~~brother~~ brothers and three ~~sister~~ sisters.
2. I work in clothing store.
3. I'm cashier.
4. I'm student at adult school.
5. I'm taking four class.
6. I have computer.
7. I work part time, twenty hour a week.
8. I came to the United States two year ago.

> **WRITING NOTE**
>
> **Singular and Plural Nouns**
> 1. Use an article with a singular noun.
> 2. Use *an* with nouns that begin with a vowel sound: *a, e, i, o,* and sometimes *u.*
> 3. Do not use *a* or *an* before proper names: *Tom, California.*
> 4. Plural nouns usually end in *-s* or *-es.* Some irregular plurals are *men, women,* and *children.* Do not use *a* or *an* with a plural noun.

D **ACADEMIC** Organize your ideas in the chart. Then, write a story to introduce yourself to your teacher and your class. For help, refer to the writing model on the previous page.

> **WRITING NOTE**
>
> Look carefully at the correct composition format. Refer to it when you write a composition.

My Family	My Work	My Interests	My Future

E In small groups, share your stories. Ask each other questions.

A Look through this textbook and complete the information. Then, share your answers with the class.

1. There are _____ pages in this textbook.

2. Look at the table of contents. There are _____ units in this textbook.
    Two topics in the textbook are _____ and _____.

3. There is a grammar chart section that begins on page _____.

4. If I need spelling rules, I can look on page _____.
    Write the third person simple present of these verbs:

    fix _____   wash _____
    cry _____

5. I can look up the irregular form of past verbs on page _____.
    Write the simple past of these verbs:

    break _____   fly _____   teach _____

> When you open a new textbook, it's a good idea to look through the book quickly. You can see how the book is organized and where helpful information is located.

B Discuss the study suggestions. Add more suggestions.

1. Grammar
    - Look at the charts and examples.
    - Write some of your own sentences using the new grammar.
    - Review any mistakes you made in class or in your homework. Write the sentences correctly.
    - _____

2. Speaking
    - Practice conversations from the unit with a partner.
    - _____

3. Listening
    - Listen to the audio several times. Write some of the sentences.
    - _____

4. Vocabulary
    - In a notebook or on your cellphone, write two or three words each day that are new to you.
    - Look up the words in a dictionary or ask someone the meaning. Write each new word in a sentence.
    - _____